# YOUNG JAZZ ENSEMBLE COLLECTION

## Piano

## Contents

*Page numbers in each book vary; therefore, each player must refer to the contents page in his or her own book.*

D1275474

Alfred

Project Manager: **Pete BarenBregge**
Production Coordinator: **Edmond Randle**
Design & Layout: **Thais Yanes and Judit Martinez**

# TAKE FIVE

By
PAUL DESMOND
*Arranged by MIKE LEWIS*

**Piano**

# SUMMERTIME
### (From "PORGY AND BESS")

By
GEORGE GERSHWIN,
DuBOSE and DOROTHY HEYWARD
and IRA GERSHWIN
Arranged by CALVIN CUSTER

**Piano**

# ON GREEN DOLPHIN STREET

Piano

Lyrics by NED WASHINGTON
Music by BRONISLAU KAPER
Arranged by VICTOR LOPEZ

# MISTY

Music by ERROLL GARNER
Arranged by MIKE LEWIS

**PIANO**

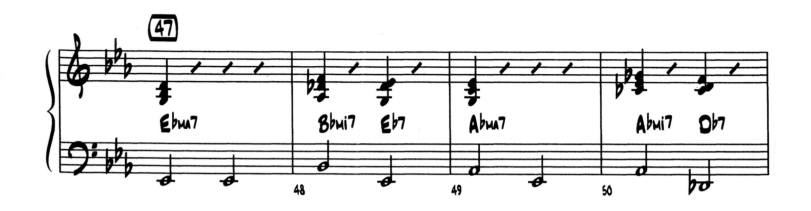

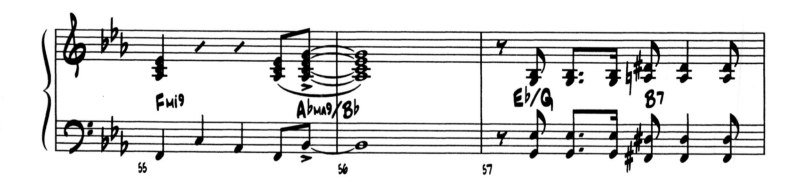

# BLUES IN THE NIGHT

PIANO

Lyrics by JOHNNY MERCER
Music by HAROLD ARLEN
*Arranged by CALVIN CUSTER*

18

# TASTES LIKE CHICKEN

Piano

KRIS BERG

# HAVE YOURSELF A MERRY LITTLE CHRISTMAS

Words and Music by
HUGH MARTIN and RALPH BLANE
*Arranged by VICTOR LOPEZ*

**PIANO**

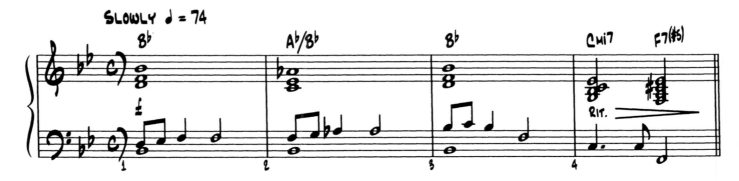

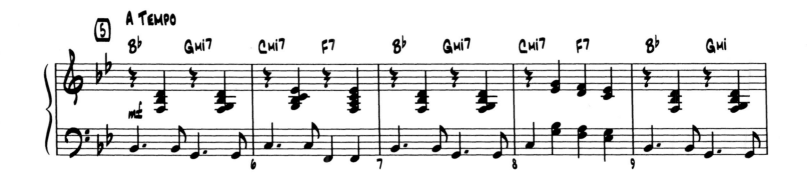

# SAX TO THE MAX

Piano

by MIKE LEWIS

# JUMPIN' AT THE WOODSIDE

PIANO

Music by
COUNT BASIE
Arranged by PAUL COOK

# JUNGLE BOOGIE

Words and Music by
RONALD BELL, CLAYDES SMITH, ROBERT MICKENS,
DONALD BOYCE, RICHARD WESTERFIELD, DENNIS THOMAS,
ROBERT BELL and GEORGE BROWN
Arranged by VICTOR LOPEZ

Piano

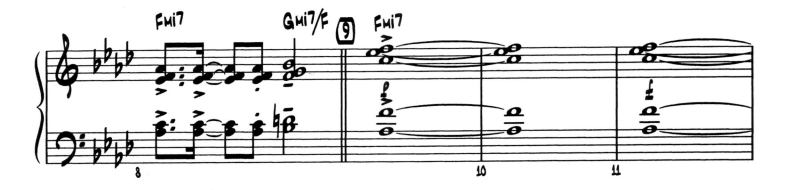

# BURRITOS TO GO

Piano

VICTOR LOPEZ (ASCAP)

38

# NIGHT AND DAY

Words and Music by
COLE PORTER
Arranged by DAVID PUGH

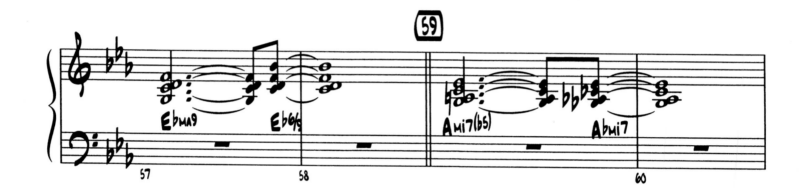

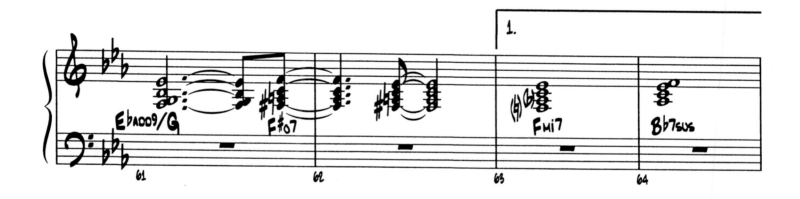

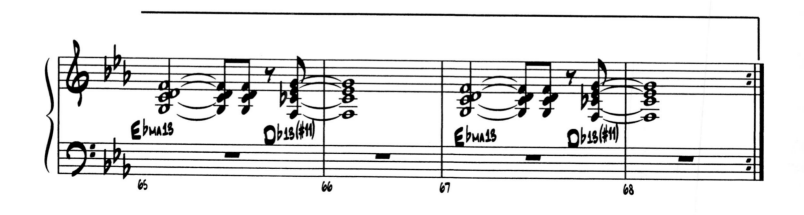